IMAGES
of America

PRESTON
COUNTY

IMAGES
of America

PRESTON
COUNTY

Charles A. Thomas

ARCADIA

First published 1998
Copyright © Charles A. Thomas, 1998

ISBN 0-7524-0930-1

Published by Arcadia Publishing,
an imprint of the Chalford Publishing Corporation,
One Washington Center, Dover, New Hampshire 03820.
Printed in Great Britain

Library of Congress Cataloging-in-Publication Data applied for

No amount of labor, research, and care

can render a work free from error or defects.

—Dr. Worcester

Contents

Acknowledgments

The great majority of illustrations in this volume are taken from the History House Archives, property of the Preston County Historical Society. All of the pictures have been gifts to the society over the years, with a special acknowledgment to the S.H. Garner's negative files that were contributions by his family.

Other sources to be credited are as follows: *Preston County of West Virginia* (1978), Morton's *History of Preston County* (1914), Wiley's *History of Preston County* (1882), Betty White's *The Past Is a Key to the Future* (1990), Alice Penzo, the Rowlesburg Area Historical Society, *A Brief Review of Preston County History* by C.C. Pierce (1939), Donnie Mann, and bits and pieces from dozens of areas of research. Added to this, a big thank you goes to my wife, June.

Introduction

Preston County, West Virginia, is the only county in the United States with that name. It is fitted into a corner of the state bounded on the north by Pennsylvania and the Mason-Dixon Line, and on the east by the state of Maryland.

The county varies in elevation from a low of 870 feet to a high of 3,236 feet above sea level. It is divided north and south by the Cheat River. The Cheat, a wild, impetuous, and rocky river with rapids and falls, claimed many of those attempting to ford; thus, it is aptly named because it "cheated" so many lives.

Preston County received its name from an established custom of naming new counties for the public men of the Old Dominion. The Virginia Assembly chose to honor James Patton Preston, then governor of Virginia, in selecting a name for the new county.

The land of Preston County as we know it today is taken from an original land grant known as the North Neck Section of Virginia to Lord Thomas Fairfax. West of the Fairfax Line, additional grants were made in 1745 of 100,000 acres and 60,000 acres. To mark property lines, one method used was known as the tomahawk rights, that is, blazing trees to mark the boundary. In 1754, grants of land were obtained from the Virginia government by the Ohio Company. One of these, a 5,000-acre grant to Samuel Eckarlin on the Cheat River, became known as Dunkard Bottom. There were few settlements beyond this of any permanency.

When the French left the Ohio Valley in 1776, Orange County, Virginia, had become unwieldy, and Frederick and Augusta Counties were formed. Monongalia County was subdivided from Augusta, and then in 1818, Preston County, Virginia, was divided from Monongalia County.

By 1776, there were 250 people in Preston. Life in these times was crude and primitive. The American Revolution was a trying time for area residents because they were isolated and because hostilities with local Native Americans broke out. After the conflicts ceased, settlers began to come again. Two forts, Fort Morris and Fort Butler, provided a haven for the settlers as late as 1785.

In 1784, General George Washington journeyed to Preston County to inspect his land holdings. Following Yorktown, Washington was interested in the development of the west and had plans for canals and highways in this section. He was mistakenly advised that some day the Cheat River might be used for water freight.

By 1767, the northern border of Preston County was marked by the famous Mason-Dixon Line. The 24-foot lane through the forest provided a passageway for the early settlers. Although some historians state that the first settlers in Preston County were the Judys in 1769; however, deed books from Monongalia County show that in 1766 Thomas Butler and his brothers arrived by the Indian Trail and settled near the Cheat River, at what was later called the Whetsell Settlement. Until the establishment of Preston as a county, the inhabitants of this territory were mainly occupied hewing homes out of the wilderness.

Following several petitions to the General Assembly of the State of Virginia, the county of Preston was formed on January 19, 1818. The population at that time was nearing three thousand. Agitation had been growing for a county seat in Preston as the distance of traveling to Morgantown for legal business was a real hardship.

After the county was organized, industry, agriculture, and roads became important. Warpaths were superseded by trails that led through the forests, allowing the exploration of the county.

One

Breaking Away

In looking at Preston County's early history, we must remember that this territory was literally locked within the mountains.

Augusta County, Virginia, part of which was to become Preston County, did not have a county government until 1745. In 1734, the boundary of Frederick and Augusta Counties was the Fairfax Line.

Virginia, with its thousands of square miles, had been divided into only eight counties. In 1734, Orange County, Virginia, was formed and took in all the territory west of the Blue Ridge Mountains. In 1776, Orange County was divided into two counties, Frederick and Augusta, and in that same year, Augusta was subdivided and Monongalia was one of the counties formed.

Industry began to appear in the 1770s as settlers arrived in west Augusta via rough trails. Many petitions were sent to the General Assembly of the State of Virginia requesting a county seat, citing the hazards of travel to Morgantown.

In the meantime Kingwood, the oldest settlement, was officially named a "town" by the General Assembly of Virginia on January 23, 1811.

Beginning in 1792, petitions asking for a new county began being filed with the State of Virginia, citing the difficulties of "crossing the ridge of mountains where there is no inhabitant, nor ever can be."

In 1795, another petition stated that the dreaded mountain caused jurors to shrink from duty. More petitions were to follow in 1799, 1800, and 1805. It required a quarter century of agitation before the General Assembly endorsed the petitions as "reasonable."

At long last, the Act of Assembly creating Preston County, naming the boundaries, which "shall form a distinct new county and be called and known by the name of Preston."

As named by the assembly, the organization of the county was to take place at Colonel William Price's Tavern in Kingwood. So, by the act of the Virginia Assembly, Preston County came into being January 19, 1818.

But the area was not without activity during the quarter century of waiting. There were roads, iron works, post offices, gristmills, and local development in progress and a population of three thousand people.

JAMES PATTON PRESTON, fourth son of
William and Susanna (Smith) Preston,
Born June 21, 1774, At "Smithfield," Mont-
gomery Co., Virginia, died there May 4, 1843.
Served as governor of Virginia from December
10, 1816 until his three years expired in December of 1819. During this period of time,
Preston County was formed, on January 19,
1818, and named for Mr. Preston a Virginian
who had distinguished himself in public
Life.

The Eckarlin Brothers were attracted by the Ohio Company to settle in the territory that the company had opened in Preston. In November 1754, 5,000 acres were granted to Samuel Eckarlin. The area where the brothers planned to establish a monastic community became known as Dunkard Bottom.

It was unfortunate that the Eckarlin Brothers chose to build their cabin so close to the Great Warpath. Native Americans raided the settlement, totally destroying everything and killing the inhabitants. A re-enactment, *Forks of Cheat*, produced by West Virginia National Public Broadcasting, portrays the Eckarlin Brothers beside the Cheat River (seen in the top photograph). Note: Eckarlin has been spelled in a variety of ways.

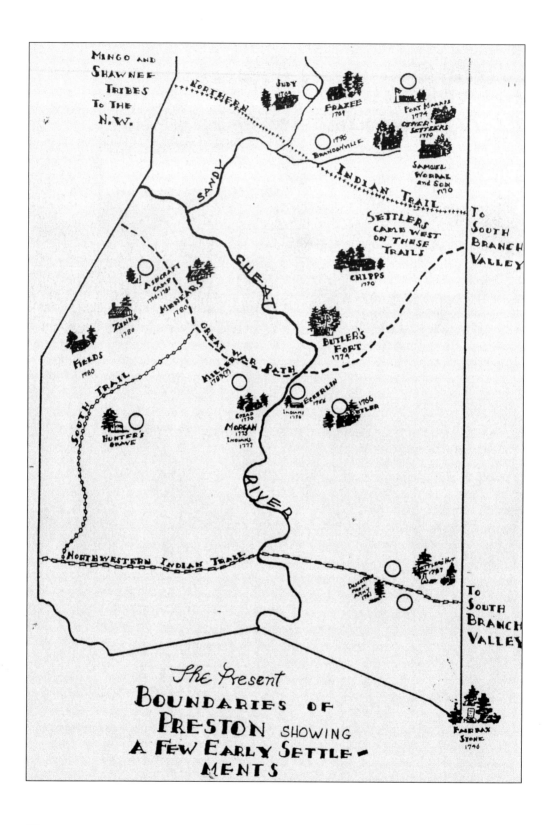

MINGO and SHAWNEE TRIBES TO THE N.W.

NORTHERN

JUDY 1762

FRAZEE 1769

FORT MORRIS 1774 OTHER SETTLERS 1770

BRANDONVILLE 1790

INDIAN TRAIL

SAMUEL WORRAK and SON 1770

SANDY

CHEAT

SETTLERS CAME WEST ON THESE TRAILS

TO SOUTH BRANCH VALLEY

ASHCRAFT CAMP 1776-1781

MENEARS 1780

ZINNS 1780

CHIPPS 1770

GREAT WAR PATH

BUTLER'S FORT 1774

FIELDS 1780

SOUTH TRAIL

MILLER 1783(?)

ECKERLIN 1766

COBAR 1770 MORGAN 1772 INDIANS 1777

INDIANS 1776

SETTLER 1766

HUNTER'S GRAVE

RIVER

NORTHWESTERN INDIAN TRAIL

DESERTERS FROM ARM 1761

SETTLERS HUT 1767

TO SOUTH BRANCH VALLEY

The Present
BOUNDARIES OF
PRESTON SHOWING
A FEW EARLY SETTLE-
MENTS

FAIRFAX STONE 1746

Fort Morris was a stockade built near Glade Farms. It was here that local families fled for shelter at the rumor of a Native American raid. These people are attending the dedication of the Fort Morris Marker in 1915. The inscription reads: "THIS TABLET MARKS THE SITE OF OLD FORT MORRIS 1774. UNVEILED AUGUST 28, 1915 IN MEMORY OF THE EARLY PIONEERS OF THE SANDY CREEK GLADES (VA) W.VA."

PROGRAM

OLD FORT MORRIS
MONUMENT UNVEILING
AUGUST 28, 1915
NEAR GLADE FARMS, W. VA.

MUSIC

INVOCATION

MUSIC

Short Addresses and Greetings from Historical Societies

MUSIC

12:30 P. M.—BASKET DINNER

2:30 P. M.—UNVEILING OF MONUMENT

Four Ladies Standing at the Four Corners, in which Stones from

GIST'S PLANTATION................................1753
(Mt. Braddock, Fayette Co., Pa.)

FORT NECESSITY................................1754
(Wharton Township, Fayette Co., Pa.)

COL. CRAWFORD'S SPRING................1767
(Connellsville, Pa.)

DR. DODDRIDGE'S FARM*................1773
(Independence Township, Washington Co., Pa.)

Are Imbedded in the Concrete Base of the Monument

ADDRESS—"DEFENDERS OF OLD FORT MORRIS"

Rev. Ellis B. Burgess, Pastor Trinity Lutheran Church

Connellsville, Pa.

MUSIC

BENEDICTION

Charles Mason and Jeremiah Dixon, two celebrated astronomers and surveyors of London, England, marked the Mason-Dixon Line in 1767. One hundred years later in a resurvey by the National Geodetic Society, it was found to be in error no more than 1.5 inches at the end of the 233-mile run. The accuracy of this survey is considered to be one of the most amazing feats in land surveying history.

One of the most beautiful vistas in Preston County displays the Alleghenies at their best. Mason and Dixon never had it so good.

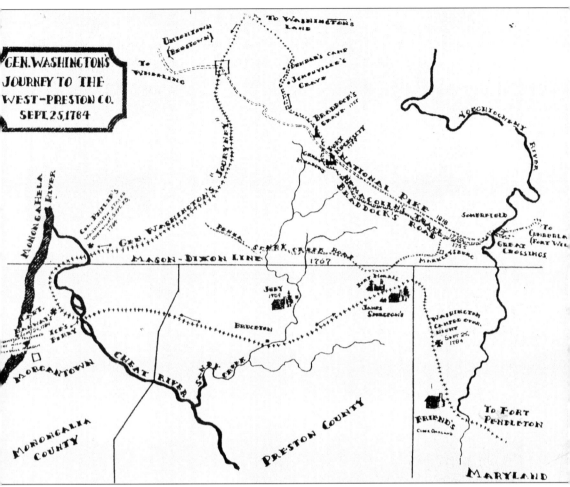

GEN. WASHINGTON'S JOURNEY TO THE WEST—PRESTON CO. SEPT. 25, 1784

Washington's party crossed the Cheat River at Ice's Ferry. They had been told that the old path to Dunkard Bottom had grown up, so they traveled northeast past Brandonville to stay overnight at the Spurgeons. They then traveled south within the Virginia border to a point on the old DeBerry farm near Hopemont for their next camp.

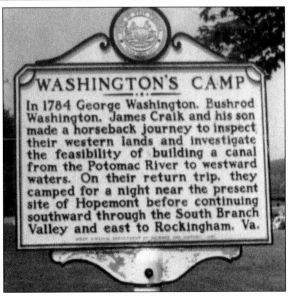

WASHINGTON'S CAMP

In 1784 George Washington, Bushrod Washington, James Craik and his son made a horseback journey to inspect their western lands and investigate the feasibility of building a canal from the Potomac River to westward waters. On their return trip, they camped for a night near the present site of Hopemont before continuing southward through the South Branch Valley and east to Rockingham, Va.

At a Court held for the county of Preston June Term 1827 — ordered that William Dragoo be allowed the sum of six dollars for killing one old Wolf as per account here filed and that the same be paid out of the county levy of 1827 —

Charles Byrne C. P. C.

At a Court held for the county of Preston June Term 1827 ordered that George hahin be allowed the sum of six dollars for one old Wolf caught & killed within the County within the preceding year as per certificate here filed and that the same be paid out of the county levy of 1827

Test Charles Byrne C. P. C.

At a Court held for Preston County June Term 1832 — ordered that James Hamelton for the use of Charles Byrne be allowed the sum of six dollars for one old Wolf caught and killed by him since the last June Term and that the same be paid out of the County levy of 1832 —

Test Charles Byrne C. P. C.

In the outskirts of the settlements, there were considerable numbers of wolves and bears. In fact, wolves became so troublesome that the General Assembly of Virginia on March 19, 1827, authorized the county court to offer a reward for killing them.

The Lutheran congregation at Aurora (Mt. Carmel) dates from the year 1787. The first building was constructed of logs and was used as both a church and a school. The second church was built in 1841, and this present structure was begun in 1890. The first building was destroyed by fire in 1845; however, the altar from this original church is still preserved and used in the Parish Hall.

AURORA

Rev. John Stough and family settled at Mount Carmel about 1787, and about 1790 Stough started the first gristmill. The first church was the Salem Evangelical Lutheran Church, organized between 1792 and 1796.

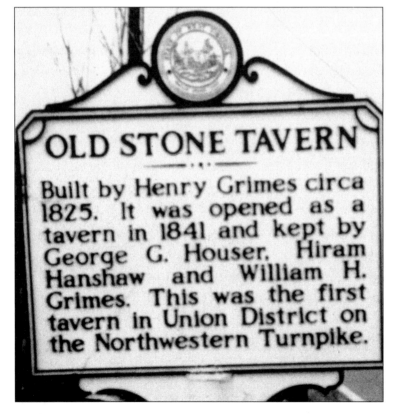

OLD STONE TAVERN

Built by Henry Grimes circa 1825. It was opened as a tavern in 1841 and kept by George G. Houser, Hiram Hanshaw and William H. Grimes. This was the first tavern in Union District on the Northwestern Turnpike.

The Old Stone Tavern on Route 50 (the Northwestern Turnpike) was built by Henry Grimes about 1825. It is located just over one mile from Aurora, which was settled as Mount Carmel about 1787. Aurora is the oldest permanent settlement in Preston County.

The Chorpenning House was built just east of Brandonville on the Brandonville Pike in 1794 by Isaac and Samuel Forman. The first newspaper in the county was printed by Frank Alters at this house in 1840 and was named *The Mount Pleasant Silk Culturist and Farmer's Manual.* Jonathan Chorpenning bought the house in 1850 and was appointed a constable in 1870.

The Cress House at Crab Orchard is the second oldest existing stone house in Preston County. It was built by Jacob Cress in 1821. Jacob was, for a brief time, a private in the Virginia Militia during the War of 1812. The house has changed very little over the years. The present owners are Mr. and Mrs. William Feather.

Fairfax Manor was built 2 miles from Kingwood on the Albright Road. Colonel John Fairfax had been the superintendent of George Washington's lands (including the Mount Vernon estate) for seven years until 1790. At that time he acquired a large tract of land in the Monongalia Glades, and between 1810 and 1815, he purchased 400 acres on the east side of Kingwood. In 1817, Colonel Fairfax began construction of this home, but it was not completed for several years.

This log house was located on the original John Fairfax land-grant estate near Reedsville. It is thought that the old log houses on the estate were originally slave quarters. Fairfax was known to have owned slaves, a practice that was customary for the landed gentry of his day.

Despite the lack of clarity, this image needs to be part of this collection. The Trowbridge Ferry was a ferry across the Cheat River at Dunkard Bottom and dates from the late 1800s. Morton states that Jesse Trowbridge, who built the ferry, came from the Shenandoah Valley in 1804. Manning the oars is an unidentified man and Lulu Trowbridge, operator of the ferry.

The first house on Roaring Creek, Pleasant District, was built by a Revolutionary War soldier, Samuel Crane, who was awarded a 250-acre land grant in 1799. Several notable Prestonians were born here, including longtime Preston County clerk Smith Crane and Orlando C. Crane of the Terra Alta Bank. The farm is often referred to as the "Old Crane Farm" by Preston County historians.

In 1918, a celebration, a picnic, and a parade were held in Aurora to commemorate the 100th anniversary of the formation of Preston County on January 19, 1818. Earl Deakins follows the sign dressed as Uncle Sam. Note that Route 50 was not yet paved.

Two

Gettin' There

At first it was a narrow path used only by pedestrians. As the footpath was worn by passage through the wilderness, it became a trail. The trail soon became a road wide enough for a single pony or even a wagon to pass over.

As one method of transportation superseded another, it became evident that east-west roads were necessary to provide a link to the western territories. Industry was making a feeble start in the area and needed an outlet to the east. General Washington had plans for roads and canals, but cautioned that "roads seemed to have been marked to promote individual interests, rather than the public good."

The first important road was the National Road (US Route 40), which ran 3 miles north of Preston County. It was the only improved road in existence between east and west, and it led to a great increase in the population of Preston County. The National Road was conceived in 1811 and finished in 1848. S.T. Wiley, in his *History of Preston County*, states "It was one of the greatest, if not the greatest, state roads ever built on the American Continent, and a marvel of human energy."

The next road of importance was the Northwestern Turnpike (US Route 50). It crossed all of Preston County and provided competition for the National Road. According to Wiley, "The advent of the Northwestern Turnpike besides inaugurating a wonderful career of material prosperity, and opening to the traveler the romantic and beautiful scenery of northwestern Virginia, was calculated to advance the intellectual, social, moral and religious interests of the communities through which it passed." Additionally, he continued, "it would increase the population by thousands and the wealth by millions." The Northwest Turnpike, which ran west from Winchester 237 miles before arriving at Parkersburg on the Ohio River, was authorized in 1827 and completed in 1838.

With the close of the year 1852, the Turnpike Period in all its glory ended and the era of railroads was ushered in. On New Years Day, 1853, the first train crossing the veritable wilderness of Preston County reached Wheeling, Virginia. The Baltimore and Ohio Railroad originated in Baltimore and soon became famous all over America.

"The Surrey with the fringe on top" was so equipped to provide protection from dust kicked up by the horse. These four ladies with broad hats, each with a different skirt length, are ready to travel. Not to be overlooked are the driver, nattily dressed with watch fob chain in vest pocket, and the patient white horse in the background. The time is before 1900, but the location and persons could not be identified.

Available to the gay young blade for courting was the single-seat buggy with a convertible top. W.K. Forman and Maggie Donaldson are attending a lot sale in Brandonville in 1912. The horses were named Goldie and Silver.

The Terra Alta Dray was operated by H.H. Hartley and is shown here at the railroad depot around 1917. The dray was owned by an independent hauler who would deliver goods from the railroad station to the store or individual to whom it was consigned. The horse-drawn dray was replaced by the Kelly Transfer, owned by Elias Kelly. The vehicle used was a Rugby truck, a long-forgotten make.

Heavy wagons and heavier horses were used for commercial hauling. The horse collars are lettered JSN Co. in brass, as are the containers on the wagon. Neither man has been identified, but the well-dressed man with the derby hat might very well be the owner of the JSN Company. This rig with its convertible top is at the Kingwood Railway Station about 1910.

This tin-type photograph is of the Kingwood mail hack that met the West Virginia Northern at the station. Passengers were also accommodated. After 1905, the hack began meeting the M and K train. No information is available about the driver or the ownership of the team.

This team and wagon stands in front of the YMCA Hotel at Lake Terra Alta. It transported luggage from the B & O Station in Terra Alta to the hotel as a service to hotel guests in 1900.

The advent of the automobile was to revolutionize travel. The Ford Model-T, with its high clearance, was very popular. This group of five are in a 1908 Model-T touring car equipped with a toolbox for repairs, acetylene headlights, side lanterns, inflatable tires, a fold-down windshield, and a top that could be pulled up in a hurry in case of rain. The license plate reads 15566 (note the hand crank, located just above the license plate).

Attorney L.F. Everhart was proud of his 1923 Model-T Ford coupe. By this time the Model-T had reached a greater degree of dependability. No need for a tool box on the running board—all the tools could be kept in the "boot." A windshield visor and windows that could be raised and lowered added to the comfort. A crank for emergency starting was still standard.

Route 50 winds up over Laurel Mountain. The Northwestern Turnpike (Route 50) to this day is the same as it was in the 1920s when it was first paved. The topography is such that it would be extremely difficult to transform it into a modern highway.

As the text on the photograph points out, the S-curves on Laurel Mountain, Route 50 west from Aurora, are very sharp and have not changed over the years. This mountain was a real challenge to the cars of the 1920s and earlier.

The Osgood Bus Lines served Morgantown and all towns on Route 7 east to Oakland, Maryland. This bus has stopped at Schwab's Drug Store on Price Street in Kingwood on a summer day in the 1940s (the drugstore was a ticket/waiting area for the passengers). The round-trip runs were frequent and dependable. Marvin (Joe) Wilhelm drove more than a million miles on this route.

The Greyhound buses of the 1920s did not ride as smoothly as a train, but they traveled to a lot of places that the rails did not. The seats were soft and the drivers courteous. Route 50 was the only highway that Greyhound or its subsidiary, Blue Ridge Lines, traveled in Preston County.

The covered bridge across the Cheat River on the Northwestern Turnpike was built by Josiah Kidwell and crew in 1834. It was approved by the State of Virginia in the following year, and was a toll bridge until after the Civil War. The two-lane structure was 339 feet long. Vehicular traffic stopped in 1934 when a steel span was built just downstream. The landmark was destroyed by fire in 1964.

The highway bridge at Caddell was originally built as a railroad bridge in 1906. Prior to that time the only bridges across the Cheat River were the bridge at Albright (1828) and the covered bridge near Macomber (1834–35).

The Bull Run Bridge over the Cheat River is approximately 1.5 miles from the community of Bull Run in Valley District. The bridge blueprint states that it was designed and built by the Canton Bridge Company in 1911. Its length is 220 feet and it has a width of 16 feet. The height above the water is more than 50 feet.

Everyone is intent on the work at hand in this picture of the new bridge crew. The time is in the early 1920s, and the location is on the railroad at Rowlesburg. A water tank for the steam engines can be seen in the background.

B & O Center Cab 2-8-0 Number 1848 waits here in the yards at Corinth. Locomotives with a cab over the boiler were called "Mother Hubbards" on some railroads, but the B & O men called them "Snappers." Pictured are R.C. Felton (in the cab) and W.F. St. Clair (with his hand on the piston). The boy on the pilot has not been identified.

It is train time at the Albright station on the Morgantown and Kingwood Railroad. The station was located in the area of the coal preparation plant. The author's wife recalls her mother sending her as a very young girl on a trip to Morgantown to visit her grandmother. Her words to the ticket agent were: "Half fare and all the way."

It did not always end well. The details of this 1915 wreck have been lost in time, but the upright locomotive is heading the wreck train with a crane and equipment. The disabled engine had been pulling a train of empty hopper cars. The accident is believed to have occurred on the Cheat River Grade, west of Rowlesburg.

This postcard was cancelled with a 1912 date, so we know that the photograph is at least that old. In 1912, the Terra Alta Railroad Station would have been twenty-nine years old. Today, at 114 years of age, it needs a lot of help. Passengers are shown here awaiting an afternoon westbound train, while eastbound passengers crossed the track to another platform.

The railroad tunnel through the mountain at Tunnelton was, when constructed in 1849–52, the longest railroad tunnel in the world at 4,100 feet. It became a constant bottleneck because it was only a single track tunnel. The new tunnel (shown here) was a double track. Completed in 1912, it was about 25 feet below the old bore with a length of 4,250 feet. The original tunnel was closed and sealed in 1962.

The Tray Run Viaduct spans the Tray Run Gorge just over a mile west of Rowlesburg on the Cheat River Grade of the Baltimore and Ohio Railroad. The original trestle was completed by 1856, and this massive stone viaduct—about 450 feet in length—was completed by 1888. The construction impressed many persons. The image of the viaduct was included as part of the design of the reverse of the state seal of West Virginia.

It took a heap of shoving to get a train over the hill. Here, Helpers No. 7100 and No. 7125 assist an eastbound manifest up the 2.2% rise into the Salt Lick Curve in August 1948. The helpers would cut off "on the fly" at Terra Alta and return to the M and K Junction.

The M and K Junction was a beehive of activity in the days of steam. All sizes of "helper" engines stood ready to lend a hand up the Cheat River Grade to the west or the Cranberry Grade to the east. The shops were able to handle heavy repairs. The advent of diesel engines greatly reduced the work force required at the shops.

A young boy studies the running gear of B & O Type EM 1 articulated locomotive No. 7600, built by Baldwin Locomotive Works in 1944. The large tenders had a capacity of 25 tons of coal and 22,000 gallons of water. The total engine and tender weight was 1,010,000 pounds. Nothing larger could have operated within the clearances on the B & O lines. Sadly, these engines are no longer in existence—all EM-1s were gone by 1960.

About 1947, just after World War II, the Baltimore and Ohio tried to recoup some of its passenger business with the Cincinnatian from Washington to Cincinnati. The train was powered by a streamlined President-class passenger locomotive and refurbished cars. It tried, but failed, to perform as a profitable passenger train. In 1950, the route was changed to run from Cincinnati to Detroit.

This locomotive was known as a Davis Camel. It was built in 1872 at the B & O's Mt. Clare shops. They were called Camels because the cab on the boiler made a "hump on its back." Originally numbered 364, this engine was renumbered 264 in 1884 when the B & O renumbered all of its locomotives. J.C. Davis was the master of machinery for the railroad—hence the name, "Davis Camels."

The Salt Lick Curve was a major engineering feat when it was first excavated and filled in 1852. Originally built for a single track, the grade at this point is 2.8%. The cut and fill were widened for a double track in 1875, and the third track was put in place in 1910. This photograph, dating from 1935, shows a coal drag with one 2-8-8-0 mallet engine at the head with an 0-8-8-0 "helper" pushing. The water tank near the helper was removed at the end of the steam era.

The West Virginia Northern Railroad began life as the narrow-gauge Tunnelton, Kingwood and Fairchance Railroad. It never got to Fairchance. In 1895, the road was purchased by George C. Sturgiss and J. Ami Martin, who rebuilt it to standard gauge and renamed it the West Virginia Northern. Regular passenger service was scheduled into the 1920s, when the automobile took its toll of railroad passengers. The line remained a freight operation until it was sold to Jim Arnold, who changed the name to Kingwood Northern, Inc. and converted the line into an excursion train, a train used for passenger pleasure trips.

The last railroad passenger service in Preston County was provided by a B & O (CSX) Amtrak Turbo Train. Use of the Turbo Train was experimental, and it was determined that it did not adapt well to mountainous railroading or heavy snow. The service was of relatively short duration.

Three
Making a Living

With courage enough to track the wilderness, the early settlers were also enterprising enough to find a way to keep body and soul together.

There was a time—known as the Transition Period—that lasted for forty-six years during which the population of Preston nearly doubled. The coming of the railroad brought many people, but greatly lessened the traffic on the pikes. The valuable home market was gone, but the railroad created another.

Preston County was primarily an agricultural county. There was an abundance of iron ore, and iron furnaces became successful. Wat Carlyle had the first iron furnace in 1815. His beginning capital was a barrel of watered whiskey, a counterfeit $10 note, and a box of homegrown tobacco. By 1839, and two owners later, the Greenville Furnace was listed as the largest taxpayer in the county. Woolen mills began in 1844 and soon there were four operating mills.

Coal mining was the backbone of the prosperity of the county. In 1853, the first car of coal was shipped from Newburg. Millions of dollars of investments were made and 4 million tons of coal were taken from that area alone.

Other businesses in the region included tanneries, salt wells, limestone quarries, shook factories, and whiskey manufacturers. Morton, in his *History of Preston County*, adds the following insight into the commerce of the county: "Rye was condensed into liquid form and became an article of export down the Ohio River. Revenue laws brought about the closing of the stills and the growing of rye ceased." Morton concludes his history by stating that, wherever outgoing Prestonians have settled, they appear to have acquitted themselves with credit, whether engaged in agriculture, industry, or in professional life.

This 1890s threshing scene was photographed before the development of the threshing machine. Two horses are on a treadmill, which by a belt operates a chaff piler. This machine separated the grain from the chaff and then blew the chaff into stacks. The grain was gathered into baskets at the base of the machine.

Oxen were occasionally used as "beasts of burden" on county farms. Here is an ox team at work doing their part to help with the threshing of grain. The nine men in this threshing crew have a huge stack of straw to attest to their hard day's work.

"Amber waves of grain" were also to be found in Preston County. Here a triple-horse team pulls the reaper. The grain is then bound into shocks to dry prior to threshing. This is a 1915 picture.

A healthy herd of Hereford cattle faces the camera in 1915 on the Jacob Smith farm in the Craborchard. Preston County has long been considered ideal for cattle raising. In early years cattle drives took place over dusty roads to the railroad and on to other markets.

Mrs. Kathleen O'Brien stands beside the hitching post of this ten-sided barn on Route One, Masontown. The barn has an interesting history. It was originally built in Monongalia County by farmers of Irish descent. Because of its location near the site of a proposed coal mine, it was moved over 40 miles to the present location. It was disassembled, each piece coded, and rebuilt at the present site. The only change was to build a covered riding track around the entire exterior.

The introduction of a local livestock auction by E.S. "Jim" Evans in the 1930s was a real benefit to the Preston County farmer. Buyers came to the auction in large numbers. This 1975 photograph of feeder calves entering the arena also shows the buyers' seats opposite the auctioneer. The auction barn is still in use on the "Stockyard Road" in Terra Alta.

The Hazelton Mill is the oldest existing buhr, or burr, flour mill in Preston County. This 1939 photograph illustrates the original mill race and waterwheel. It is to this day the chief supplier of buckwheat flour to the Buckwheat Festival. Presently, however, power for the buhrs is a gasoline engine.

The Eglon Roller Mill is one of the two gristmills still in operation. It utilizes steel rollers to grind grain as opposed to stone burrs. Built in 1911, it is powered by mechanical means rather than a waterwheel.

The Bruceton Grist Mill was located on Big Sandy Creek in Bruceton Mills, and was important to farmers for a long time as a well-operated mill. There were at least five buildings on the site, this one built in 1904. Originally water powered, it operated for many years under several owners and operators. The mill's dam is all that remains of the big mill, which burned in 1952.

Gristmills took advantage of the gravity system to transform grain into flour as depicted in this photo of the circular grinding buhrs. The grain traveled down a chute from the upper floor, into the hopper above the buhrs, and then down into the buhrs themselves. The flour emerged on the next floor down.

The iron industry in Preston County flourished for a period just before and after the Civil War. Furnaces, such as the Virginia Furnace (shown here), located near Ruthbell, were built in areas where iron ore was found to exist. Charcoal was used for fuel, and a nearby stream furnished power for the blast. Harrison Hagans of Brandonville built this furnace in 1852. The iron produced was hauled by wagons to Terra Alta for shipment by rail to Eastern markets. Also known as the Muddy Creek Furnace, the operation closed in 1880.

About the time that Preston County was formed, Andrew Ochiltree and James Caldwell built the Valley Iron Furnace. The stack is still standing and is located just above present-day Lake-of-the-Woods. They used the Cheat River and New Geneva, Pennsylvania, as their market outlets; consequently, transportation difficulties led to the abandonment of their enterprise.

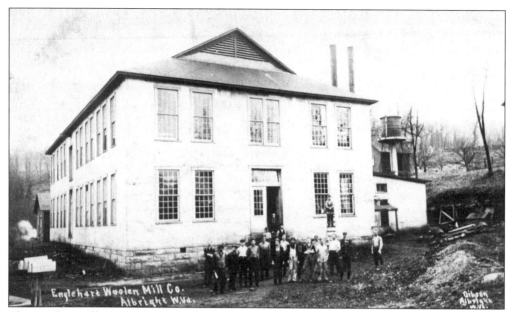

The woolen mill on Muddy Creek was bought by John Englehart in 1888 and became the Englehart Woolen Mills. The mill was expanded to house twelve looms. Raw wool was processed into woolen fabric for blankets and clothing. Distinctive dyes were developed and used here. Later, the mill burned.

Charles Spindler was a general contractor in Preston County in the period following World War I. He specialized in road building and excavation. A steam shovel (actually operated by steam) is shown here working on a county road building project. In later years Spindler was elected sheriff of Preston County.

Coal mining has been one of Preston County's most important industries. In 1855, the first coal mine opened at Newburg. During its thirty-five years of operation, over 4 million tons of coal were taken out of the Pittsburgh seam. In recent years, as seams have been worked out, the volume of coal mined has diminished. For nearly fifty years Newburg was the largest and most prosperous town in the county.

Many coal mines were not as roomy as the interior of this Preston County mine. To the left is the motor (engine) that pulled the rail cars through the mine. Note that each miner has his own carbide lamp on his hat. In many smaller mines, miners could not stand erect.

Mine car 5329 with an old-style mine-car motor, "Camel Jack," is pictured here in 1900. the horse Camel Jack had been pulling mine cars continuously for forty-two years according to Grant's *Photo History of Preston County.*

By 1900, electric motors were used to haul coal from the mines. As can be seen in this photograph, power was transmitted through an overhead trolley wire. This 12-ton electric motor hauled the coal from mine to tipple (the place where the coal car were tipped) for the Merchant's Coal and Coke Company of Tunnelton.

Hundreds of thousands of tons of coal were extracted from the hills around Masontown. Some coal was shipped and some was converted into coke and then shipped to the steel mills. The coal was carried by conveyor from the mine to the top of the tipple and then dropped into bins for loading into railroad cars.

The Preston Coal and Coke Company had extensive operations at Cascade on Decker's Creek, about a mile from Masontown. The coke ovens illuminated the night sky with a fiery glow. Shut down in the 1950s, the ovens were to be idle and cold forever.

The bar on the track in front of this Shay engine was placed there as a safety measure. These company houses were the homes of workers for the Rowlesburg and Southern Lumber Railroad, located near Erwin. It is probably Sunday afternoon because the men are in suits and hats and most of the ladies are in white dresses.

The Shoemaker sawmill was one of many small family sawmills that cut and processed virgin and second-growth timber in the county. It was hard work cutting the timber with a two-man crosscut saw, dragging the logs to the mill with teams of horses, and firing a steam boiler to operate the circular saw.

The Rodeheaver sawmill, crew, and equipment on Beaver Creek was typical of a late World War II–era lumber company. Most of the men are older, past the age for military service. Note that the two-man crosscut saw was still in use. The gasoline chain saw was yet to come.

This view shows a small portion of the Morrison-Gross lumber yard in Erwin. The mill was located on US Route 50 at the foot of Cheat Mountain. The Rowlesburg and Southern Railroad connected the two communities and also followed the river upstream for several miles to bring timber to the mill. In the 1920s, it was the largest lumber operation in the county.

The town of Manheim was built by the Alpha-Portland Cement Company as a place of residence for their employees. There were at least fifty-four homes, plus a superintendent's home, a clubhouse, a post office, and a school. As can be seen in this picture, a neater company town would be hard to find.

This "dinky" railroad was built up high on the mountain where limestone was quarried for the Alpha-Portland Cement Company at Manheim. The "dinky" hauled the stone from the quarry to the chutes. From that point, gravity took the it straight down to the crushers. The company was proud of its record number of years without a lost-time accident (an accident that causes an employee to lose time, or be absent from work, for treatment of injury).

This small gasoline engine replaced the former steam "dinkies" at the quarry of the Alpha Portland Cement Plant at Rowlesburg. There was a network of tracks linking the limestone mines with the chutes to the crushers. It was dusty work!

The Alpha Portland Cement Company was located at Manheim just north of Rowlesburg on the M and K Railroad. The mountain above the plant was virtually all limestone. The stone was quarried at the top of the mountain and dumped down long chutes to crushers at the bottom. Many carloads of cement were shipped from the plant each day.

One of the projects of the Works Progress Administration in the early 1930s was this sewing room located in Kingwood. Pictured with the workers are rows of sewing machines, a quilting frame, ironing boards, and stacks of blankets and pillows. The exact location remains unidentified, as do the workers.

The West Penn Power Company was one of the early suppliers of electricity to Preston County. As the utility evolved, a portion became the Monongahela Power Company. Pictured here in the late 1930s is Mr. John Collins and the line crew on the steps of the Inn in Kingwood.

Pryor's photo of the Mike Kelly Fruit Store in Rowlesburg is a real gem. Presumably, Mr. and Mrs. Mike Kelly are standing in the center, obviously solid patriotic citizens. Their location on the railroad would have enabled them to have a reliable supply of perishable fruits and vegetables by Railway Express even at the turn of the century. (Mann.)

Scott's Drug Store in Terra Alta was located in the first K of P building, which was built prior to 1920. S.M. Scott Jr., the owner, is pictured here to the left with Frank Downer, telegrapher for the B & O Railroad. The business still continues in 1997 as Gregg's Pharmacy.

The C.W. Forman-Jacob Smith store in Lenox on the Brandonville Pike is the oldest continuously operated store in the county. Built and opened in 1882, it has been in operation ever since. C.W.'s son, W. Klet, operated the business from 1926 until his death in 1962. Since that time the William Bolinger family has owned and operated the store.

The Great Atlantic and Pacific Tea Company was the first—and for a long time the only—corporate food chain in Preston County. A strictly cash policy gave them a sharp competitive edge over the traditional credit and delivery merchant. Typical of their stores was the store on Price Street in Kingwood. In 1997, the Kingwood supermarket, the last A & P in West Virginia, closed its doors.

The Bank of Kingwood was the first bank to be chartered in Preston County. It was organized in 1865 with capital of $100,000. William G. Brown was the president and James C. McGrew was the first cashier. It evolved into the Kingwood National Bank, then into the Albright National Bank of Kingwood, and eventually became Wesbanco, today's bank.

The Terra Alta Bank was organized in 1891, and this brick structure was begun in 1892. This is the oldest surviving bank in the county. In 1991, the bank outgrew this location, and the building was then given to the Preston County Historical Society. It now houses the History House, the museum of the Preston County Historical Society, and is listed on the National Register of Historic Places.

The First National Bank of Terra Alta opened its first office in 1903 in a room of the Offutt-Lakin Building. Charles A. Miller was the cashier, and James S. Lakin was elected president. In 1907, they built a three-story structure on the northeast corner of Main and State Streets. Pictured in this 1902 photograph are W.H. Harriman (left) and C.A. Miller.

The First National Bank of Newburg was organized in 1905 with J. Clay Smoot as cashier, and the bank grew with the town. As a national bank, it was sufficiently strong to back national currency imprinted with its name and officer's signatures. When the coal industry in the Newburg area declined and the Great Depression of 1929 took its toll of the economy, the bank was forced to close.

The People's National Bank of Rowlesburg was built in 1912 to serve the communities of Rowlesburg, M and K Junction, Manheim, Erwin, and surrounding rural areas. D.W. Wiles, cashier, (on the right) is pictured with a group in front of the original building.

The Bank of Masontown was chartered about 1910, when the Elkins' interests began developing Decker's Creek Valley by purchasing coal lands and constructing the M and K Railroad. The bank served the area until 1932, a victim of the Great Depression and a declining coal economy.

The town of Tunnelton was impressive in appearance in 1900. Just to the right of center is the two-story Baltimore and Ohio Railway Station. Left and to the rear of the station is a three-story mercantile building. The railroad tunnel is about one-half mile up the tracks to the left.

In February of 1868, a town meeting was held in the railroad community of Simpsons Water Station and the name was officially changed to Newburg. Because of its location on the grade to Tunnelton, the B & O installed a "helper station" and wye in the center of town. The Newburg-Orrel Coal Company operated a large coal and coke oven operation here. At the height of its productivity, Newburg was the largest town in the county. Here, on January 21, 1886, a mine shaft explosion killed thirty-nine men, which was to that date the largest coal mine disaster in the nation.

Four

Flashback

It has now been 213 years since General George Washington put Preston County "on the map."

History tells us that in 1784 George Washington rode across the north and east of the county where he had claim to more than 49,000 acres. He and his party traveled through the September rains stopping with such folks as Captain Hathway, Mr. Lemon, Colonel Zackwell Morgan, John Evans, and John Spurgeon. Thirty years earlier Washington had passed over the Braddock Road, just to the north, and he now returned as an interested observer of the country. According to Morton's *History of Preston County*, "The glades called forth his admiration and he remarked how the roads could be bettered." Hence, the beginning of the linking of the Eastern Seaboard with the interior.

Preston was too sparsely settled for any organization, and a substantial village was slow to arrive. In 1793, Deakins and Hogmire plotted the town of Carmel. The site included a public square with a courthouse. The earliest school was also at Carmel.

The pioneers were observers of the phases of the moon, and they had their "signs" for planting, butchering, and other matters; without due heed, the undertakings would not prosper. A belief in the flatness of the earth was general. Even in sunlight hours, "spooks" and ghosts appeared in the countryside.

However picturesque and romantic the pioneer period might be to read about, the settlers likely considered it dull and commonplace.

Rowlesburg, on the Cheat, has long been a prominent part of the county. Its location on the river aided its growth over the years, but the river has also caused much heartbreak and destruction due to floods. At one time, Rowlesburg was the largest town in the county, and it may have held that title when this photograph was taken (it had to have been taken before 1910 because the twin Bollman Truss railroad bridge, visible in the distance, was replaced by a

This courthouse was built in 1870 after the previous one was burned in 1869. There was an effort to move the courthouse to Cranberry in late 1869 (see Wiley, p. 102), but the board of supervisors directed that the $8,000 of insurance money and all salvageable material be used to build on the old location in Kingwood. The building served its purpose for sixty-three years. It was then replaced by the present courthouse, dedicated in 1934.

double-track Warren Truss bridge that year). The smoke rising in the distance, to the left side of the picture, comes from the B & O Railroad shops. There is a mountaintop behind the photographer's location called Cannon Hill, so named because Union forces placed cannons there to protect the railroad during the Civil War.

MAIN ST. KINGWOOD, W.Va.

Courthouse Square, fronting on Main Street in Kingwood, is where the Soldier's Monument and the Civil War cannon are mounted. The cannon was last fired in defense of Fort Sumter, South Carolina, in 1861. It was hauled by three teams of horses from the railroad station and placed in the square in 1912. A pyramid of cannonballs displayed with the cannon disappeared one night in 1932. The Soldier's Monument, dedicated in 1903, and the cannon take up a 40-foot square area leased to the Grand Army of the Republic in 1895 for ninety-nine years.

Albrightsville, later shortened to Albright, was on the Cheat River with the only river bridge between Terra Alta and Kingwood. In this picture there are two hotels, one of which is the Bishoff House, on a short unpaved street. Albright was named for David Albright, but the first house and business was built in 1840 by William Morgan.

Meet Elijah E. Alford, who came from the state of Maine and built the first house in Terra Alta in 1840. He acquired land, and in anticipation of the coming of the railroad, marked lots for sale in the town of many names. When a post office was established in 1849, Alford was the first postmaster of Salt Lick Falls, which was to become Portland, Cranberry, and finally Terra Alta.

Lloyd G. Beerbower and Charles W. Beerbower left the farm at Glade Farms in 1891 to join the "pilgrim band" of Professor H.N. McGrew of Philadelphia. The band traversed considerable territory in the states of Maryland, Pennsylvania, Virginia, and West Virginia, selling illustrated editions of John Bunyan's famous book, *Pilgrim's Progress*. They also gave evening lectures with the help of a stereopticon viewer. After working under McGrew for some time, the Beerbower brothers acquired their own wagon, pictured here.

Photographed in the late 1890s, this is a rig with a Preston County history. The entire outfit was once the property of the Fairfaxes. The buggy was made in Morgantown in 1858. The mule is Sweet Sixteen. Grant, in his *Photo Record of West Virginia*, says, "Samuel has the distinction of having honorably served his country during the late unpleasantness." Samuel was a Fairfax family slave until he was emancipated during the Civil War, or the "late unpleasantness."

In 1921, two men developed a rather brazen scheme to rob the bank in the little farming community of Bruceton Mills. Somehow, the plot was discovered, and they were met with loaded guns. Dr. Dafoe, shown here with the rifle (or shotgun), wounded the man on the ground. The other man had his suspenders severed with a bullet and could not run. It is said that he saw the error of his ways.

The Alms House at Kingwood was commonly known as the "Poor House" or the "Poor Farm." Operated by the County, it provided a home for the indigent who had no place to live and no income. The present welfare systems have modified the need for such a facility. The Preston County High School is now located on many acres of this property.

The Honorable James C. McGrew was born near Brandonville on September 14, 1813. He spent much of his youth in that area of Grant District. In 1833, and for the next thirty years, he became involved with many enterprises throughout Preston County. He married Persis Hagans, daughter of Brandonville's Harrison Hagans, in 1841. He was nominated as a delegate to the 1861 Virginia Convention, which was to vote on secession. A strong Unionist, he voted against secession and became unpopular with the majority. He and his companions were forced to return home from Richmond secretly. In 1866, he was the cashier of the National Bank of Kingwood. In 1868 and 1870, he was elected a member of Congress from the Second District of West Virginia.

In Wiley's 1882 *History of Preston County*, there are forty-two references to James C. McGrew. In addition to his business, civic, and patriotic work, he found time to build this magnificent house. It became a home for many social events. Presently in Kingwood, the McGrew Society is endeavoring to restore this home to its former grandeur. The house was built in Kingwood in 1841.

The Terra Alta sign still stands, but the "Airport" sign is long gone from the intersection of Route 7 and the Brandonville Pike in Terra Alta. In the 1930s, the second building was referred to as the Mason House (in a previous time it housed an undertaking establishment). In the late 1940s, the A.R. Dodge Service Station was still in business. It was also apparently a good year for weeds.

This photograph of the Forman Field hangar at the Terra Alta airport dates from 1948. Forman Field was so named because the land was purchased from J.H. Forman, a local farmer. Charles Bohon and Kenny Smith formed the Mountaineer Aviation Service. They had the runways graded, and with only three aircraft, they started a flight-training service. There was insufficient demand for such a service, however, and the operation was discontinued in December 1948.

The Cottage Inn was built by Harold B. McCrum in the 1930s, complete with tourist cabins and a restaurant. It was located on Route 50 near Aurora just before Abernathy's Gulf Station. During World War II, when gasoline was rationed and people could not drive to the mountains for vacations, the cottage business declined. After the war these cabins were sold individually. Some were moved and others were combined to make small houses.

Judge Vail of Cleveland, Ohio, built the Brookside Inn about 1880. It became the top summer resort in Preston County; its clientele included the social and political set of Washington. Along with the attractive inn was an immense stable in which at least twenty-five well-groomed riding horses were kept for the convenience of the guests. One of the most successful operators of the inn was Emma Jane Kirkpatrick, who conducted the inn from 1900 to 1924.

This is the New Howard Hotel, located along the tracks in Rowlesburg. The rear portion of the building was the Hooton House until after the Civil War. The front of the hotel with the mansard roof was added in 1900. Doctor and Mrs. Howard purchased the hotel in 1925, and a new era dawned. In short order, Mrs. Howard became proprietress of what became the most revered hostelry on the entire B & O System.

Mrs. Annette Howard owned and operated the New Howard Hotel in Rowlesburg from 1925 to 1975. The hotel faced directly on the Baltimore and Ohio Railroad tracks and soon became the most revered home away from home on the entire B & O system. Her food was legendary and assuaged the hunger of guests for fifty years. Health forced her to retire in 1975, and she died in the early 1980s.

The James Brown residence, or the Inn, on Main Street, Kingwood, was built as a residence by James A. Brown in 1857 with bricks made in Kingwood. James Brown was an attorney and subsequently became the prosecuting attorney for Preston County. The home is presently used as a comfortable inn and dining room operated by Joe and Rosemary Bernatowicz.

The Hotel Raleigh stood on Main Street, Kingwood, just to the west of the sheriff's office. It was dismantled just after World War II, and the Alpine Theater was built in its place. The theater later became the home of the County Extension Office.

The home of the West Virginia YMCA Training School and Camp was the YMCA Hotel at Lake Terra Alta. In 1906, the hotel and camp was described as being one mile from Terra Alta on the main line of the B & O Railroad, 2,800 feet above sea level with cool nights, pure mountain air, and beautiful scenery. It was promoted as being the most beautiful spot in West Virginia to spend a summer vacation.

Highland Cottage was located on a hilltop in Terra Alta. In the years preceding air conditioning, hotels in the area played host to persons of means, who were sometimes able to get away from the sweltering heat of the Eastern cities. Highland Cottage enjoyed a heyday from the 1890s to the 1940s. The landmark was destroyed by fire on January 31, 1962.

Five

We Proudly Present

"Both justice and decency require that we should bestow on our forefathers an honorable remembrance." This is a quote from the Greek historian Thucydides, and so we proudly present some of the persons that Prestonians have been privileged to know and to share in a bit of their lives.

The local history of the county is personalized, and the influence of individuals looms large in the picture. It is important to remember, though, that often the activities of only a few influential individuals have resulted in the movements so crucial in the history of Preston County.

The county was more than a portal to the Great West. It lies at the very intersection of the border lines between the East and West and the North and South. A further description of West Virginia, which naturally includes the county of Preston, states the following: "The southeast can include West Virginia, although we are classified as the most eastern of the midwestern states, most northern of the southern states, and most southern of the northeastern states." Morton goes on to say in his *History of Preston County* that "Preston is a strategic point for studying the 'making of the American.' There is an intermingling of the Cavalier, the Puritan, the Quaker English, of the Scotch-Irish, the Germans, the French, Welsh, Dutch, the Celtic, and later the Italian."

The pioneers deserve ample credit for their perseverance and persistence, and the transformation they set in motion. Daniel Webster reminds us that "respect for our ancestors elevates the character and improves the heart."

On May 27, 1938, President Franklin D. Roosevelt came to Arthurdale to deliver the high school commencement address. His special train traveled from Washington to Rowlesburg on the B & O, then up the M and K branch to Arthurdale. Among those traveling with the president were Mrs. Roosevelt and FBI Chief J. Edgar Hoover. Security for a president was not so intense that day, as the proud and happy people crowded to see their president.

Mary Virginia Keck was valedictorian of her senior class at Arthurdale High School in 1942. Her father was Harrold Keck, principal of the school at that time. Mary Virginia went on to earn a metallurgy degree at Penn State University. In the photograph she is being congratulated by Mrs. Eleanor Roosevelt.

During the 1930s, Mrs. Eleanor Roosevelt was a frequent visitor to Arthurdale because of its status as a Government Homestead Project. Her friend, Doris Duke, one of the world's richest women, sometimes visited the project with Mrs. Roosevelt. Mrs. Roosevelt is shown here sitting in the automobile. Walking toward the car is Doris Duke, while the press photographers are busy capturing the moment.

The Arthurdale Assembly Hall in the community center was reconstructed from the old Reedsville Presbyterian Church, which was moved to that location. Also housed in the center were a co-op store, a barbershop, and a health center. This 1997 photograph shows the recent revitalization of the building.

The West Virginia highway marker on the east side of Arthurdale (Route 92) tells the objectives of the "pet project." The marker on the above right explains the early ownership of the area. The 2,400-acre project that was adopted by Mrs. Eleanor Roosevelt received her support, influence, time, and money.

The Arthurdale Homestead Project was established in 1933–34 by the federal government in an effort to help unemployed coal miners and their families become self sufficient. Fifty years later, many of the original homesteaders and their families gathered for a reunion to celebrate the silver anniversary of the project.

United States Senator John D. Rockefeller IV (Jay) has made many trips to Preston County both as the governor of West Virginia and as a senator. He is pictured here making a point in one of his talks on May 11, 1976.

In 1967, a somewhat younger Secretary of State Jay Rockefeller served as the coronation official at the Preston County Buckwheat Festival. He is shown crowning Lynn Taylor, Queen Ceres XXVI.

A relative returning from the West was the occasion for the Ridgway family reunion at Evansville in the 1950s. Names were furnished by the late Senator A.L. Reed. From left to right are as follows: (front row) Rachel Hamilton, Wade Hamilton, Jennie Reed, Thomas Ridgway, Nettie Ridgway, Lot Ridgway, Henry Ridgway, Rose Weaver, and Douglas Hebb; (second row) Virginia Reed, Wallace Reed, Jean Mann, Lizzie Hamilton, Archie Reed, Beatrice Reed, Alston Reed, Edna Ridenour, Paul Ridenour, Clarice Ridenour, and Lottie Hebb; (third row) Neil Reed, Reed Ridenour, Madge Reed, and Ada Ridenour; (back row) George Reed, Clarence Shroyer, Henry Hovatter, Martha Hovatter, Arthur Reed, Lulu Reed, and Ray Hebb.

This is Sam King, whose goal might be to grow the world's longest beard. Extending to the floor and past his foot by several inches, he has our vote. Photographs like this one, which dates from the 1890s, may be seen at the History House, Terra Alta.

Harriston Hagans was born in Vermont on June 17, 1796. After a short sojourn in Indiana, his family settled on the Cheat River in 1815, and then moved to Brandonville in 1818. Hagans built this stone house in Brandonville next to his store in 1830. He was an outstanding entrepreneur in many fields, from retailing to iron furnaces. Many roads and turnpikes owe their existence to his fund-raising efforts. He often contributed to the Brandonville Academy and the church.

When Mahlon Loomis died in 1886, he must have been a disappointed man. Although Congress had authorized $50,000 to support his research and had approved formation of the Loomis Aerial Telegraph Company, he was not able to raise the additional funds that were needed. He is buried on his brother's lot in the Terra Alta Cemetery.

The present home of the George Delauder family in Terra Alta was once the home of Judge George Loomis. Judge Loomis's brother, Mahlon Loomis, also lived here for some time and conducted many wireless telegraphy experiments from mountaintops in the area. It can be truthfully said that his work and experiments preceded those of Marconi, who is generally credited for the discovery of wireless telegraphy (radio) signals.

A group of Methodist men from Terra Alta chartered this special car on the Baltimore and Ohio to attend services by the evangelist "Billy Sunday" on March 9–10, 1912. Pictured, from left to right at the Wheeling Station, are (fifth) C.B. Linger, (sixth) Hansel Taylor, (tenth) O.W. Ringer, (sixteenth) D.L. Wotring, (twenty-second) J.W. Whittaker, (twenty-fifth) Cloyd Crane, and Lloyd Beerbower (fourth on the car).

In the Newburg Cemetery is the grave marker of Thomas Moran, born in County Galway, Ireland, in 1821. Many Irish emigrated to the United States in the early to mid-1800s and found employment in the coal mines and on the railroads.

In the late 1930s, Clem Teets of Terra Alta was a teacher in the Fellowsville School. One day, when he was driving on Route 50, traffic was stopped because a vehicle ahead had caught fire. When one man exited his chauffeur-driven car, Clem had to look up, and up, and up. The passenger was Robert Wadlo of Alton, Illinois, the tallest man in the world. He measured in at over 9 feet tall. Robert did not live to an old age. There is a full-size sculpture to his memory at Southern Illinois University near his home.

The Americana Museum in Terra Alta is an outstanding collection of Americana. It was brought together by Clem and Ruth Teets of Terra Alta. One of the many buildings in the museum collection is this log cabin. Mrs. Bessie Goff was there to demonstrate how the spinning wheel, the loom, and other items were used.

The Hopemont Tuberculosis Sanitarium was authorized by an act of the West Virginia Legislature in 1911. It was located on the crest of the Allegheny Mountains because fresh, unpolluted air was the best known remedy for T.B., as tuberculosis was commonly called. From left to right you can see the dairy farm, the nurses' residence hall, Gore Hospital, the post office, Conley Children's Hospital, the dining hall complex, and patient cottages.

This view of Hopemont looking west pictures the dining hall complex and patient cottages. The cottages were designed so that patients' beds could be wheeled to an outside porch for maximum sunshine and fresh air. After a cure for "TB" was found, the hospital was converted to other uses. It is now shared by the Valley Mental Health Center and a care home for the elderly.

Mr. L.S. Bucklew was a musician, cabinetmaker, historian, and collector of artifacts. He was a member of the Knights of Pythias, a popular fraternal organization in the period around 1900. As shown in the photograph, the uniforms were patterned somewhat like the Union Army uniform of the Civil War. The musicians' uniforms also compare to the Union Army musicians. This picture was taken in Kingwood.

This comely young lady with her hat is appropriately posed before photographer Gatz's floral background. The year is 1890, and her elaborate dress and demeanor suggests she was born to refinement.

Six

Worthy of Honor

There are stories to tell about the patriots. In the summer of 1861, it was reported that fifteen hundred Confederates were on the way to Preston to blow up the Baltimore and Ohio Railroad bridge at Rowlesburg, the Kingwood Tunnel, and to do other damage to the railroad.

General William Jones's efforts to destroy the railroad in Rowlesburg were thwarted by a Rowlesburg resident warning Jones that he was greatly outnumbered. However, in Fellowsville and Evansville the raiders did burn bridges and loot area stores. One soldier took much feminine apparel and tied it to his saddle. Jones made the soldier dismount, put on one of the skirts, and parade up and down the street. He was reproved for loading his horse with merchandise that could do him no service.

Meanwhile, at Terra Alta the Confederate soldiers were moving through and capturing most of the citizens who had been bravely helping Captain J.M. Goodwin and his squad.

M.F. Stuck, a deputy sheriff, was one of the citizens in the skirmish that was captured. Stuck was defiant! Hands tied behind his back, he was ordered to mount a stump to be shot. (Confederates and Federalists were instructed to execute any men in citizen's clothes found to be firing upon troops.)

No one knows why a change of order was given by Colonel Harman not to shoot Stuck. He was put hatless on a bareback horse, forced to ride 3 miles out of town, and was told by Colonel Harman that he would be tried in Richmond for treason. Stuck was then released and Colonel Harman told him never to get caught again.

The legend in Terra Alta says that from the stump, Stuck made a Masonic sign to Colonel Harman that was recognized, and this recognition of the "sign" by Harman is credited for sparing the life of Mathias F. Stuck. When asked how he got away from Harman, Stuck said it was a matter between the colonel and himself.

When we think of patriots, no group comes to mind sooner than the Boys of 1861–65. Whether they volunteered or were drafted, they served the Union. In the photograph each man is numbered. Somewhere there must be a roster matching the numbers and names. This picture was taken near the Inn in Kingwood about 1920.

Little information is available regarding the number of draft calls in Preston County during World War I. This call on May 25, 1918, was larger than the number in the photograph. These fellows had only five months and seventeen days of war to face; still plenty of time for combat.

Thirty-six Preston County boys from Board Two are ready to take the bus to the Waldo Hotel in Clarksburg, where they would be given physical and mental examinations. More than one half were deferred—of the thirty-six pictured here, only seventeen were ordered to report to Fort Hayes on November 17, 1942.

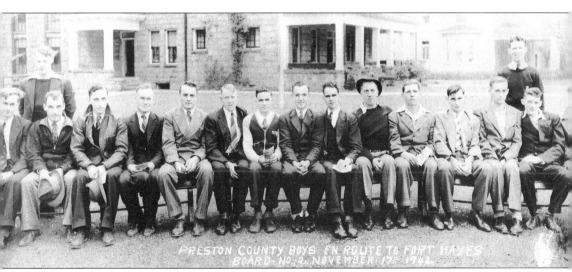

These Preston County boys are en route to Fort Hayes, in Columbus, Ohio, from Board Two, in November 1942. After being picked up in Kingwood, they traveled by bus to Tunnelton, boarded the B & O for Athens, Ohio, and then changed to the New York Central for Columbus and Fort Hayes, where they received uniforms and assignments.

The most demanding conflict the United States ever became involved in was World War II, and Preston County's Draft Boards furnished a constant stream of recruits from 1941 to 1946. Above is the "call" for October 30, 1942. This was the last group sent to Fort Thomas for uniforms and assignments.

The number of draftees called from Board Two on January 5, 1943, was only twelve, a much smaller group than usual. These men could look forward to three years of military life, if they were lucky.

In March 1943, minimum age for the draft was lowered from twenty-one to twenty. These boys are on their way to Clarksburg for examinations. Boards One and Two covered different geographic areas of the county. This photograph of the draftees was taken by Preston County photographer S.H. Garner.

These boys, from Draft Boards One and Two, are headed for the examination center at the Waldo Hotel in Clarksburg. Their ages varied from nineteen to thirty-seven. By this date, younger and older age groups were being drafted.

The National Guard has long been popular with men of military age in Preston County. Pictured is the Terra Alta Company in the early 1920s at the intersection of Washington and Main Streets awaiting transportation to Camp Dawson. At this time their headquarters in town was on the third floor of the Offutt-Lakin Store.

The Civilian Conservation Corps (CCC) was a government program developed in the early 1930s to provide employment for rural youth during the Great Depression. It was organized on a semi-military basis; all members wore uniforms and lived in barracks. Their work was to plant trees, build roads, and perform other forestry conservation-related work.

Camp Dawson was established on May 7, 1909, when the legislature authorized the purchase of 196.5 acres of land on Dunkard Bottom along the Cheat River in Preston County. The camp was named in honor of Governor William M.O. Dawson, a native of Preston County. Troops began training at Camp Dawson in the summer of 1909, and continued until the start of World War I. Because training was then suspended, the camp was not used again until 1928, when Governor William G. Conley appointed Carleton C. Pierce of Kingwood as the state adjutant general. Camp Dawson was then reestablished as a training site for the West Virginia State Militia (National Guard). The present total acreage is 1,487 acres.

Check this successful sky jump demonstration at Camp Dawson. One important job that is done at Camp Dawson for the Army is the repacking of "jumped" parachutes. This job requires highly skilled specialists. From time to time the parachute packers are required to make a jump using a repacked parachute. This is the best insurance to guarantee that the job has been properly done.

This photograph of Mr. and Mrs. M.F. Stuck and their son shows the family when he was proprietor of one of the hotels in Portland (Terra Alta). Mr. Stuck was associated with other businesses and was also a deputy sheriff. An account of his activities at the time of the Jones's Confederate raid is given in the introduction of Chapter Six (p. 85).

Susanna Miller Albright (1791–1867) was the wife of David Albright, for whom the town of Albrightsville (Albright) was named. They came from Pennsylvania to the Albright area in 1810. Susanna typifies the hardy pioneer woman who faced the unknown for a chance to carve her own place in the frontier.

R. Doyne Halbritter was born on June 7, 1902, in Reno District near Tunnelton. He attended Tunnelton schools, West Virginia Wesleyan, and West Virginia University. He entered the field of education, but later earned a law degree and began the practice of law in 1936. His greatest interest was in county history and genealogy. He was one of the founders of the Preston County Historical Society, and at the time of his death in 1976, he was president of the society. In later life he devoted much of his time to county history and welcomed many family researchers who sought his guidance.

William G. Conley was born near Kingwood on January 8, 1866. He graduated from West Virginia University in June 1893 with a degree in law. He practiced law for some years and was a Republican candidate for Congress in 1912. The election was lost by a mere fourteen votes. He entered the gubernatorial race in 1928 and became West Virginia's eighteenth governor.

Samuel Haymond Garner was born in Preston County near Kingwood in 1880. About 1900, he became an apprentice to Kingwood photographer D.L. Martin. In 1904, Mr. Garner purchased Mr. Martin's business and the Garner Studio was established. Mr. Garner was to remain THE county photographer until his death in 1950. Quite a number of the photographs in this book were taken by Mr. Garner, and were gifts to the Preston County Historical Society from his family.

Charles E. Trembly passed to his reward twenty-seven years ago, on March 28, 1970, at almost ninety-seven years of age. After an early teaching career, he became the assistant cashier of the Terra Alta Bank, and continued with the bank for the next sixty-eight years. In the growing years of Terra Alta, he was instrumental in forming the electric company, the waterworks, and the first telephone company. He was involved in the organization of many county businesses and held office in many civic groups.

Educator, farmer, businessman, humanitarian, and philanthropist—W.R. Shaw was all of these. When he died, he left an endowment to be used for civic improvements in the town of Terra Alta. The town hall, the Shaw Memorial Football Field, Fireman's Field, the fire department headquarters, the ambulance squad building, the town garage and recycling center, and many other improvements were made possible by the Shaw Fund.

Harriet, daughter of John P. Jones, was nine years old when her family came to Terra Alta. At age twelve, she entered Wheeling Female College and upon graduation, entered the Women's Medical College in Baltimore. She graduated as a medical doctor in 1884, the first female doctor in West Virginia. Her first practice was in Wheeling, and for twenty years she operated a hospital for women in that city. Dr. Jones was instrumental in establishing the Salem Industrial School for Girls, the Hopemont Tuberculosis Sanitarium, the Denmar Tuberculosis Sanitarium, the State Children's Home in Elkins, and domestic science in the public school curriculum. She is buried in the in the Terra Alta Cemetery.

This placard of candidates in the May 1932 Primary Election in Preston County is a non-partisan slate with fifteen Republicans and two Democrats. The Democrat steamroller that elected Franklin D. Roosevelt to his first term was to come with the November election of 1932.

Seven

For the Mind and Spirit

In 1865, a system of free schools went into effect taking the place of the subscription system, which began about 1790 and in which the parents paid for school, suggesting that education was a private matter. Until 1796, any school in the area was the result of private effort.

There was only one family to each 4 square miles—a population too sparse to enable a school to exist. In 1796, the Virginia Legislature passed a law that all children would have free tuition for three years. This law was advisory rather than mandatory, and no use was made of it in Preston. However, three men were appointed to "look after" education, and when a section of the county had enough children to form a school, a decision could be made. Some taxes, called the Literary Fund, were denoted to encourage education. By 1850, there were forty-two common schools and 840 students. By 1879, there were 126 schools in the county with 3,548 pupils and an average monthly salary for teachers of $28.84.

County institutes conducted by experienced educators were held regularly. During this era of growth the need for higher education was sorely felt. Few could go away to school, so two academies were established: the first was the Preston Academy in Kingwood in 1841, and the second was established in Brandonville in 1843. These schools did much to promote the cause of education.

Oren F. Morton's *History of Preston County* tells us that "Although the desire for religious freedom led to the founding of more than half of the American colonies, it would be in great error to suppose that the American people were generally religious at the time the settlement of Preston began."

About 1786, the Friends began a place of worship in an old house in Brandonville. A Quaker church was later built in the same area. In 1787, the Salem Lutheran at Mt. Carmel was built, the first church house to be built in the county. Beginning in 1798, denominations of the Methodist (1798), Baptist (1800), Dunkard (1836), Presbyterian (1840), Holy Roman Catholic (1845), United Brethren (1873), and Amish (1871) were organized.

According to Morton, "Effective preachers were known to have stentorian voices which could be heard long distances, and when 'wild man' Reverend Samuel J. Clawson talked about the abode of the lost he became so fiery and so realistic as to make the hair of the listener stand on end."

The oldest school photograph that we have been able to obtain is of the Bruceton Mills School of 1883. The name of the teacher is unknown, but relatives have identified two of the pupils as Dessie Feather and Charles Beerbower.

The roof is the limit in this picture of the Reckart School in 1909–10. This school was located on the Orr/Cuzzart Road. Imagine the discipline required for this group of young men. The first person in the first row to the right is Foster Cuppett, who later became a teacher for many years. The competent teacher is Amos Wolfe.

The Lick Run School was on Lick Run just a stone's throw from the Brandonville Pike near the Craborchard. Mr. S.G. Nester was the teacher in 1911–12. In the center of the back row with a button-down sweater is McKinley Cramer; to his right is his sister, Mildred Cramer. Mr. O.Z. Gibson was a photographer who lived and worked in Lenox and each year made the rounds of the schools for an annual picture.

The year 1910 was a good one for Rachel B. Deets as the teacher of the school at Amboy, located close to Aurora on the Aurora Pike. It was necessary to have good discipline and a good sense of humor for a lady teacher in 1910, and "Miss Rachel" qualified.

Center School was nearly a mile from Lenox off the Brandonville Pike on the Cuzzart Road. Artie O. Metheny was the teacher in 1914–15 of the twenty-nine students in grades one through eight. There was a spring of water close to the school and plenty of grapevines to swing from.

In 1916–17, the Sugar Valley School had thirty-one students in grades one through eight. Amos Wolfe was the teacher, and beside him is his son, Glen. The Sugar Valley School was between Valley Point and Bruceton Mills on what is now Route 26.

The Tunnelton Public School was built in 1914 complete with a belltower. This beautiful brick building accommodated grades one through twelve. The student body is gathered for a "last-day-of-school" picture.

The school building at Mt. Nebo was a two-room school with white pillars and cement steps. The grating over the windows was a protection from baseballs, not the threat of vandalism. The school was located just off the main road from Valley Point (Route 26). Mrs. E.S. Pell was the teacher in 1914–15.

The tallest student in the center of the back row is Harvey Cale. This picture shows the pupils at the Cale School in 1917–18 with Jessie Jenkins as the teacher. In the bottom picture, you will find Harvey S. Cale as the teacher at the Glade Meadow School, just one year later (1918–19). He continued as the teacher there the following year, and the number of pupils doubled.

Upon completion of the elementary program, a student could take summer courses at a county normal school and become qualified to teach. Also held at certain of these normal schools were teacher institutes to provide refresher courses. Harvey S. Cale was a student at the Cale School in 1917–18, and was hired as a teacher at the Glade Meadow School in 1918–19 after completing a term of Summer Normal School.

This group of ladies and gentlemen comprise the Summer Normal attendees at Terra Alta in the year 1903. After six weeks of intensive study and testing, a person could be awarded a temporary teaching certificate.

By 1913, there was much demand for Summer Normal School education and training. The Terra Alta Elementary School, built in 1901, was a commodious institution and a favored location for Summer Normal.

The Brandonville Academy was authorized by the Virginia Legislature in 1843. Harrison Hagans of Brandonville introduced the legislation. It operated as an academy until after the Civil War. The school was built in 1843 with bricks made in Brandonville. During the Civil War the building served as headquarters for Company C, 3rd Regiment, West Virginia Cavalry.

The Preston Academy in Kingwood was authorized by the Virginia Legislature in 1841, and the building was completed in 1844. It served as an institution of higher learning until 1874. Terms were five months long, with April and October being the months of vacation.

At one time, every magisterial district in the county had its own high school, with the exception of Pleasant District. Here is the Grant District High School at Bruceton Mills in 1919–20. Seated on the ground, to the left in the second row, is Principal Lynn Waddell.

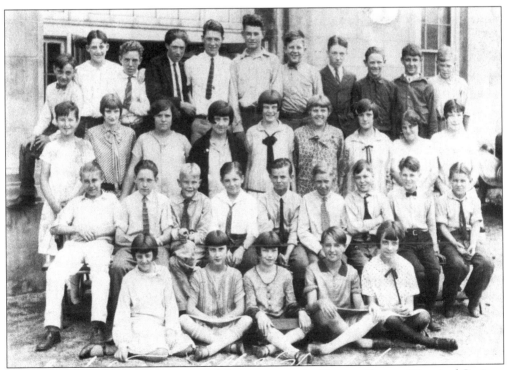

Lucian McDaniel of Fairmont presented this picture to the Preston County Historical Society. His class in 1926 is posed in front of the newly completed Terra Alta High School.

HIGH SCHOOL, KINGWOOD, W. VA

The Kingwood High School was built in 1874 after the Kingwood Academy had closed. It served as a high school for fifty years. When the present Central Preston Junior High building was constructed in the 1920s, this building became the Kingwood Elementary School. It was demolished in the 1970s. The location was on High Street, Kingwood.

PRESTON CO. TEACHERS INSTITUTE AND FORMER TEACHERS

This august group of teachers and former teachers were gathered for the summertime Teachers Institute at Kingwood. The year was 1930, and D.K. Mason was the superintendent of schools. The Teacher's Institute was not a new affair; it had been observed since 1909 at Terra Alta for what was known as a week's review.

Graduation ceremonies from sixth grade included a group picture. D.K. Mason was the principal of the Kingwood Elementary School in 1939. Some Kingwood folks may find themselves or acquaintances in this picture.

Summers McCrum Jr. succeeded D.K. Mason as principal of the Kingwood Elementary School. Smiles and "bobby socks" appear in this sixth-grade graduation picture in 1946–47.

A country church needs a steeple, and this steeple on the Stemple Ridge Methodist Church was built to point the way to Heaven. It is an outstanding example of the art of church construction. The congregation dates to 1874.

The Eglon Maple Spring Church of the Brethren was organized in 1856. The present church building dates from the early 1900s. In a previous time there was a pool formed by the stream to the rear of the church property that enabled total immersion baptisms. The late Mrs. Lulu Fike Watson was baptized there.

The Brandonville United Methodist Church was organized in 1819 by Reverend George Hagans. It was the first Methodist church in Grant District. On Christmas Day, 1850, this stately colonial-style brick church was dedicated, replacing a frame building. In 1920, after the brick structure was determined to be unsafe, it was dismantled and the present church took its place.

For many years the grounds of the Albright Baptist Church provided an ideal setting for family reunions. This church was organized in 1834 as the Muddy Creek Baptist Church at the home of Abraham Elliott. The Elliott family still gathered there in 1908, as seen in this photograph.

There are indeed many children in this picture honoring Children's Day in 1908 at the Beech Run Church. It was the custom for the children to present the program and worship service for the day. This picture indicates that the young people had the support of the entire congregation. The Beech Run Methodist Church in Pleasant District was established in 1883.

The Kelly family gathered at Centenary for a family reunion *c.* 1920. The Kellys trace their ancestry in Preston County back as far as the War for Independence. The Centenary church has been replaced with a modern brick structure.

The Lutheran Church, near Lenox, was built in 1832, and served both a Lutheran and German Reformed congregation. Regular services continued until 1916, but at present only memorial and other special services are held. It is believed to be the oldest church building still standing in Preston County. The oldest grave in the adjacent cemetery belongs to Isaac Ervin, a Revolutionary soldier who died in 1814.

The baptism by immersion shown here is being witnessed by a large crowd of onlookers. The Allie Graham farm pond near Valley Point was used by the Mt. Moriah M.E. Church for the baptisms. The church at Valley Point was established in 1904, around the time that this photograph was taken.

The village of Clifton Mills is 2 miles north of Brandonville in Grant District. The construction of a gristmill was the beginning of the village. A post office was built in 1874, and the Union Church was erected in 1879. In 1881, John Barnes built the three-story building next to the church, which has recently burned. The little white church still serves the community.

The Albright Methodist Church Youth Choir in 1940 received encouragement and training from Mrs. Myrtle Crane (far left, middle row), Mrs. Lucille Morgan (center, middle row), and the Reverend Paul Maness (far right, middle row).

112

Eight

Fun and Games

When the time came for recreation you could choose a family reunion, playing ball, boating, swimming, a parade, a train ride, a picnic, or hiking a mountain—and all this was only a beginning. Summertime was best. No longer restricted by the weather, Prestonians were "out and about."

More entertainment could be found at barn dances with the fiddlers, home-town bands, local stage productions, the 5¢ nickelodeon, sport hunting and fishing, baseball teams, and camping trips, just to name a few.

In 1908, there began one of the finest amusement parks in the eastern United States on the Morgantown and Kingwood Railroad line near Masontown. Known as Oak Park, it had roller coasters, a carousel, and a Ferris wheel, in addition to rowboats for rent, a lovers' lane, ball fields, souvenir booths, restaurants, and hotels. There were picnic tables to accommodate 1,500 people. Many social events took place here, including church groups and family reunions. Some people came just to enjoy watching passengers get off the train. Oak Park no longer exists.

The oldest Fourth of July celebration in the state began in 1895 at Terra Alta Lake. Hundreds came by horseback and buggies. There was a small paddle-wheel steamboat on the lake for excursions at a reasonable price. A hotel of spacious and grand design, a two-story pavilion, gazebos, boathouses, and an ornamental bridge were there for the guests and visitors. An outstanding summer event was the Old Soldiers Picnic, which was the forerunner of Terra Alta's July Fourth celebration. The celebration continues today.

The Preston County Buckwheat Festival began in 1938. It was designed as a simple homecoming to be held in the fall of the year to share the beauty of the hills. Thousands came and the festivities have expanded each year to include parades, exhibits of agriculture products and livestock, adult and youth exhibits, three coronations, a pet show, an antique car show, an arts and crafts fair, and, of course, a carnival of renown. It has all the amenities of a state fair, but it just might be that the biggest drawing card of all would be buckwheat dinners. Now in its fifty-ninth year, the festival is Preston County's greatest attraction.

Stem Rock is located in the area called Camp Rocks on Snaggy Mountain, about 5 miles from Terra Alta and less than 100 yards from the Maryland Line. It was popular as a place for Sunday outings in the early 1900s. By 1930, it had become less popular and rattlesnakes inhabited the area. A forest-fire tower was built close by, and climbing it afforded a magnificent view for miles in all directions.

Cornwell Cave on the Cheat River, about 2 miles east-northeast of the community of Herring, is the largest cave in Preston County. The entrance, a small opening in a low limestone cliff, 200 feet above the river, opens into a maze of interlacing passages. The drop into the river gorge is very steep. The group of explorers in this photograph from the late 1800s includes Eddie Cornwell (standing at the bottom, third from left), who discovered the cave.

As the sign says, there were 100 acres to enjoy at Oak Park. It was owned and operated by the Baltimore and Ohio Railroad and the Elkins Coal and Coke Company. At the peak of its popularity it was considered to be one of the finest amusement parks in existence.

The Oak Park Hotel, while not pretentious, provided adequate facilities for dining and lodging. Many families visited the park for day-trips only, but bed and board was available for those wishing a longer stay. Changing transportation, a cutback in the coal economy, and the Great Depression forced Oak Park to close in 1930.

Oak Park, built in 1908 near Masontown, featured two roller coasters, a carousel, a Ferris wheel, tennis courts, games of chance, hot dog stands, rowboats, picnic tables, and ball games, just to name a few of the entertainments. Oak Park had it all!

Those brown bottles on the picnic table are the carbonated beverage of sarsaparilla flavor, pleasing but non-alcoholic. Sunday picnics were a most popular form of recreation during the summer. No further identification of this picture is available.

Balloon flights were a popular part of summer holiday celebrations. Here a crowd gathers on July 4, 1910, to watch a balloon take flight. The passenger is not visible in the photograph, but several men kneel around the base, presumably securing it.

A brave balloon passenger dangles from a parachute, which in turn hangs from the hot air balloon, at this time clearing the mountain. A large crowd watched this balloon ascension at Rowlesburg on July 5, 1909.

A parade is forming on Jackson Street in Kingwood, July 4, 1910. Kingwood was hosting a Fourth of July celebration. The band disbanded and headed north on Price Street, as the following picture indicates.

Here the parade is in complete disarray on July 4, 1910, in Kingwood. The Brown building has been decorated for the event, the unpaved street is filled with people and horses, and the trees seem to be in the middle of the street. The object on top of the Brown building is actually the courthouse cupola.

There is total confusion in the mix of parade units and spectators at the 1912 Fourth of July celebration in Terra Alta. The location is the junction of Ringer Avenue and Aurora Street. The three-story building on the left is the Offutt-Lakin Store, which burned in 1926. On the right is the three-story K of P building that preceded the five-story one built in 1923. The float of the Terra Alta Bank is the only one distinguishable.

This photograph is one of several existing photographs depicting the homecoming celebration parade of August 14, 1930. The location is East Washington Street, Terra Alta. In the foreground is E.C. DeBerry driving his unusual triple team of horses. The buildings, from left to right, are the Linger Building, the Cale Brothers Store, the L.B. Parrack Store, the Beerbower-Zeller Building, the Bosley-Wright Bakery, and the five-story K of P building. Across Main Street is the Bandstand Pavilion.

The year is 1941 and Queen Ceres IV is Dorothy Brown of Arthurdale. The Buckwheat Festival Coronation service in 1941 was under the direction of the Business and Professional Women's Club of Kingwood. The coronation official was the Honorable M.M. Neely, governor of West Virginia.

Scott Miller had the honor of being chosen the first King Buckwheat in 1938. Scott entered the Air Force in World War II and was a member of a heroic bomber crew.

This handsome Dodge sedan is decorated for a Buckwheat Festival parade not long after World War II. The Dodge Furniture Company was located off Court Street in Kingwood. The float is being driven by none other than Mr. Dodge himself.

The location of this *c.* 1915 parade and the sponsor of this decorated-car float have been lost in time. The Model-T sedan with the three young patriotic passengers was decorated to the hilt with two doves fastened to the top of the windshield. The photographer was W.R. Loar of Grafton.

Floats of every description were entered in the various community parades. A goal of the Womens Christian Temperance Union was to urge young people to sign a pledge not to imbibe in any alcohol beverages. Some did, some didn't.

It may have been a play or a pageant, but it is difficult to guess what these girls have in mind. Each seems to be trying to outdo the other in dress. The time is 1900, and the program had to do with the Terra Alta Methodist Church. From left to right are Dessie Feather (Davis), Flora Jenkins, Lona Crane, Lottie Jackson, Pearl Feather, and Margaret Parsons.

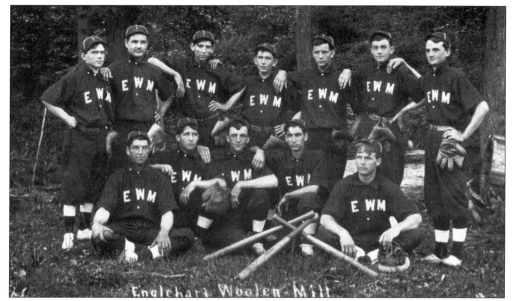

Men's baseball teams were very popular in the years from 1900 to World War II. Many businesses sponsored teams and the rivalries were great. This Gibson photograph shows the Englehart Woolen Mill team of 1909. The mill was located in Pleasant District between Deep Hollow and Centenary.

The "Alta's" baseball team was Terra Alta's finest. The best estimate of the year is 1910. The members of the team included Pat Fraley, Frank Downer, Charley Brown, Perry Windell, Cecil Lamb, Junior Sypolt, Stanhope Scott, John White, Ross Fichtner, and Joe Fox.

About 1940, Masontown was home to the baseball team of the Austin Powder Company. Dressed in their uniforms, they are posing with their mascots, two young ladies labeled Quality and Service. They are pictured with enough explosives to blow them all the way to Morgantown.

These swimmers are at the lower end of Lake Terra Alta on a beautiful summer day in 1938. From left to right are Charles Thomas, Ray Zeller, Tom Zeller, A. Zeller, Dave Bennett, Burton Thomas, and Jim Dodge.

On the shore of Lake Terra Alta was Camp Lakewood, later known as Camp Galilee. It operated as a summer camp for boys and was staffed by members of the Staunton Military Academy, Staunton, Virginia. Here on the boat docks are one hundred (count 'em) campers and staff posing for a photo.

Camp Lakewood was almost sixty years old when this photograph was taken in 1964. Over the years it has also been known as Camp Terra Alta and Camp Galilee. One hundred campers and staff are seated on the steps of the building that started life as the YMCA Hotel at Lake Terra Alta.

The rapids of the Cheat River have given rise to a new tourist attraction, whitewater rafting or boating. Rowlesburg and Albright have become headquarters for this water sport. Many of the boat operators conduct trips on other rivers throughout the state with May through October being the most popular months.

In the late 1970s the Rotary Clubs of Preston County hosted a study team from Australia. A rafting trip down the Cheat River was one bit of recreation that was afforded them. The whitewater raft is negotiating the rapids and was soon to dump one of its passengers.

The coach of this Kingwood High School football team was George Harrold Keck. He and his wife, Mary Elizabeth, came to Kingwood in 1924. Harrold taught math and served as the coach until 1933.

J. Roy Lipscomb was appointed principal of the Rowlesburg Schools in 1942. Principal Lipscomb (proudly standing in the front row to the far right) is shown here posing with the 1942–43 Rowlesburg River Lions basketball team. When Preston County had ten high schools, the River Lions were always a team to be dealt with in athletic and academic competitions. The coach is Homer Brooks.

Typical of Preston County winters is this scene on the Cranesville Road at Cupp Run. This photograph was taken during the winter of 1939–40. In 1944, a tornado completely destroyed this beautiful grove of pines.